LIFE AROMA

(FEEL YOUR LIFE WITH HEART TOUCHING POEMS)

AADYA BHARGAVI

Made with ♥ on the Notion Press Platform
www.notionpress.com

DEDICATION

I dedicate this book to my Grand Parents who constantly inspire me in my study.

I also dedicate this book to the editor Mr. Harekrushna Behera, who is my father and a great guide to me and also to my mother Mrs. Nirmala Sahu, who has guided me a lot and inspired me to write these poems.

Contents

Contents

Contents

Preface

Our feelings have no parameters. When feelings open their door, poems automatically enter. These poems are really out of the tranquility of the poet's mind. Though a poem is just like a piece of writing, inspires thousands. Whenever inspiring thoughts enter my serene mind and heart, I start penning in my diary. This book consists of 50 poems which are out of my continuous writing and patienceful editing. I hope, these poems would surely inspire thousands to go ahead in their life to achieve something new. The poem book tells about the ideas like the beauty of nature, parents, friends, family, relatives, and neighbours. This book is named as "Life Aroma" which may spread the fragrance of beauty and joy among all. After all, this book is best for all to read and enjoy; and enthusiastically share their fun with their family.

-AADYA BHARGAVI

Acknowledgements

I would like to thank my parents for their constant inspiration and guidance towards the publication of this poetry book 'LIFE AROMA'. I would also thank all my planetspark teachers for their guidance.

About The Poet

Aadya Bhargavi

The author is a young poet, one among the feelers of this mundane world. She is from Odisha (India). She loves English and poem to write. Her poems touch the hearts of people as she writes and inspires. She is the recipient of many awards for creativity and innovation. She dreams for a better Earth, where people will live happily and peacefully.

1. Oh, God!

Oh, God! Oh, God!
You are our Lord,
You are in our bodies,
That's why we can study.
You are everywhere,
On the hills, on the mountains.
You help us every time,
That makes our life a rhyme.
Oh, Lord! Oh, Lord!
You are in the form of a soul
Within me and among all
To achieve our goal.
You give us the power to think,
'I can do anything'
'Everything is in my hand',
Accept, it may be a loss or gain.
You come into my mind,
When I do meditation.
I fulfill all my dreams
With your complete inspiration.

***

2. The Autumn

Leaves falling from the trees
During the Autumn
Makes it all bare.
They all shed down
And fall without care.
And again the flowers bloom,
When the spring spreads its breeze.
And then I understood the secrets behind
"Why autumn comes?"

***

3. The River

When I was small,
I saw something blue and long.
I smelled it, it was very clear.
I heard it going shew-shew.
I felt it, it was very cold.
I tasted it, it had no taste.
I saw it, it was very big.
I then asked my father,
He said, it was a river.

***

4. Oh, Trees!

Oh, Trees! Oh Trees!
You sprout your leaves.
You give us food,
And also wood.
You give us air,
That we take with a dare.
You take the carbon dioxide,
That we release outside.
You are living things,
And we are living beings.
You provide us with vegetables...
That we eat on big tables.
As you give the fresh air...
The whole earth depends on you,
Oh, Trees! Oh, Trees!
We cannot live without you.

***

5. Chocolate I

I saw the dark one,
I saw the white one too.
It smelled so delicious that,
I heard watering my mouth so deep
That it was a bucket full.
I felt it very soft.
I tasted that and it was so yummy,
That I fell in love of
But when I saw it, it was just a
Chocolate!

***

6. Birthday

It's 12 years since my birth,
Right at this time, I was born.
I can remember when I was crying,
For a small catch, I was trying.
The day came when I was
the smallest kid for a second.
I started to cry when I came out,
My mother was happy to see me shout.
I was fit and fine
till one month
But when I went out off the road,
I started to catch a cold.
Like this, it became one year,
And again I had a day for cheer,
My parents and I
were on cloud nine...
as
it was my birthday...
Since that day again I felt good,
as I was growing older and older.
And one day again a year came
when I was two.

I spent my whole year
At the start of the study,
And when I was two and half
I had a good buddy.
And then I started
going to school
From the beginning, I was feeling cool.
And then it was again my birthday...
And no sooner I was three
This time I called up my friends
And all I had, was just fun!
I received a lot of gifts.
When my birthday was over
I was feeling blue,
but my friends encouraged me
to cheer up and cool!
This is how
I became 12,
By solving the hurdles.
The number of difficulties I faced,
Was just a great bundle.

***

7. Books

Books are my best friends,
I read them holding in a line.
Books are so fun.
They make my days done.
I know the new things which I haven't learnt.
Books tell us history,
Books tell us a story,
Books bring glory to my life.
I love them,
I show them,
I bow them
With great might.
They are the loving things
In my life.
They are non-living things.
But, they can change our life.
With different names,
They have excellent fame.
I see them.
I show them.
I watch them.
I bring them.

I buy them.
I read them.
I love them.
I borrow them.
But, they didn't give
Me any sorrow.
"I LOVE BOOKS VERY MUCH".

***

8. A Day

It was a nice and amazing day,
that, I have never wondered about.
It's quite beautiful in May.
As it was my first day in the world.
A little warm in the afternoon,
A little sunny throughout the day,
made my whole day
full of sun's rays.

***

9. Clouds

The beautiful clouds in the sky,
Seems like a big cotton candy.
With white and black colours,
Pink and orange
when it hides the ball of fire.
It brings the dusky sky
To see the children
Playing in the park and
Becomes black
To watch everyone dance in rain.

***

10. Do Birds Play?

I was in the playground,
Holding the basketball
As it got lost.
I searched all over.
I looked up to pray to God
And I was astonished
To see the ball in the hands of the birds.
I got shocked as they were playing.
Do birds play?
I called up my friends but none came,
When I opened my eyes
It was just a dream.

***

11. My Favourite Photo

The cool breeze is going on,
On the heater to get warm.
The snowballs are getting form,
Then the peaks filled with snow.
On and on we go,
The place is just Manali,
Click! Click! Sally...
There's white and white all around
So never touch the ground.

***

12. Holi

Oh! I am full of colours
Black, blue, red, purple, green
And endless colours on my body
Oh! I am totally wet out of purple.
Fun with water guns
On such an occasion.
I wish you a Happy Holi !

***

13. Be Choosy

A friend may be Faithful,
A friend may be funny,
A friend may be loving,
A friend may cheat,
A friend may fight,
A friend may argue,
A friend may be bad,
A friend may be competitive
A friend may be a foe.
No one knows what a friend is,
So, choose your friend wisely.

***

14. Fried Rice

Yummy fried rice,
Tasty fried rice,
I like its taste.
Yummm!
Full of vegetables and rice,
Shining with all its glaze.

***

15. Chocolate II

Sometimes as dark as coal,
Sometimes white-like teeth,
They are all chocolaty
And yummy indeed.
All children like that,
Yummy for me too,
If the classroom will be a fish market,
Then all students will take
And say 'yaa-hoo'.
Yes! That's chocolate,
Funnier and yummier,
They make our days and night,
Dark and bright.

***

16. God

The temple bell stopped,
Still, I can hear the sound.
God is still with me,
And I can feel him all around.

***

17. Grandparents

My grandparents are generous.
They are always on cloud nine.
They never let us feel blue.
They give us so beautiful gifts.
They teach us many things.
They bless us with their blessings.
They shower love on us every day.
They bless us to live 100 years.
G is for greatness.
R is for richness.
A is for awesome.
N is for nice.
D is for delightful.
P is for patience.
A is for admirable.
R is for rare.
E is for effective
N is for notable.
T is for truthful.
S is for sacrificing.
Let us prostrate them.
As they are our God.

18. When I Grow Up

I want to be a scientist,
When I grow up.
I want to invent the medicine for cancer,
When I grow up.
I want to cure all diseases,
When I grow up.
I want to invent a space suit that would never melt,
When I grow up.
I want to fulfill the scarcity of water,
When I grow up.
I want to fulfill the need of fossil fuels,
When I grow up.
I want to do every impossible thing possible,
When I grow up.

***

19. Happiness

Be Happy,
Don't be sad.
Be Delighted,
And be glad.
Be thrilled,
Be overjoyed.
But
Don't be dismal or
Feel bad.

***

20. The Temple At The Hill

I am very happy at the hill
The temple is there
But the bell is still.
I can calmly feel
The breeze of air
I am very happy at the hill.
I went to the temple on the hill
To meet the God
But the bell is still.
I was sleeping by a tent on that hill
When I found some new friends
I am very happy at the hill.
God is blessing me at the hill.
And I began to pray.
But the bell is still.
I thank god for taking me to that beautiful hill,
With awesome breeze
I am very happy at the hill.
But the bell is still.

***

21. If I Were In Charge Of The World

If I were in charge of the world,
I would have made the world
Full of respect and cleanliness,
Passion and profession,
Literacy and educated people
To teach the poor kids.
I would also have made
The price of very expensive things less
Like petrol and diesel,
Phones, tablets and computers
And
There would have been less
Price for the ornaments too.

***

22. It's Cold

What a cold I caught!
I felt very bad.
Just filled up with
Sneezing and coughing
Made me feel very sad.
Passing time by only sleeping
Was not so nice.
Still, I was feeling in my nose
Like there are many running mice.
But they were all
The mucus and the cough
Which made me very uncomfortable.
For that, I was suffering from
A little bit of a fever.
But when I was okay
I started counting the days.
It took me seven days
To be fully okay.
Now I can run and play
And also get some sun's rays.
It's better now and
I am very happy with my health.

23. Let's Remember

When I see outside,
I remember geography.
When I see inside,
I remember science.
When I see my mind,
I remember Einstein.
When I see myself,
I remember the whole world.

***

24. Mom And Dad Say

Mom and Dad say: Wear a mask before going
Outside to do a task.
Mom and Dad say: Use sanitizer
And always be wiser.
Mom and Dad say: Keep a 1-meter distance
In India and France.
Mom and Dad say: Always live at home. Don't go anywhere
If a stranger will say 'come'.
Mom and Dad say: Always obey us and you can ask your friends
About this fuss.

***

25. Moon

The structure full of
Dust and rocks
Has many craters
On its surface because
Of the meteorites.
The moon has been smiling
Throughout the whole night
And playing with the children
Silent and quiet.
The moon doesn't want
Anyone to know that
She is playing
With the children so.
The moon calls
The twinkling stars
And says on the phone
'Hello, come here and play'.

***

26. My Cute Sister

A naughty and cute girl,
Always makes me a fun
For her quick acts and pacts,
I have to follow her and run.
Beating and biting me often,
For small small events that happen
As she always feels 'great!'
But I have to keep my patience
And make my mind peace and set.
My pencils, erasers, books and copies
All she takes and plays
For which I can't study
And run after her all day.
All the chocolates and chips,
That father brings from the market.
She comes fast and hides these all.
There is no chance to achieve my goal.
I play a joke and fight,
With this cutest girl with all right
That makes my days fun and done.
She is the little sister of my own,
Whom I love and don't feel alone.

27. My Dad

My Dad, My Dad,
You are not bad.
I love you and
You care for us.
Dad, you teach us,
Dad, you help us in
Reaching our goal.
You are not only our God
BUT,
You are our big Lord.
Oh, Dad! Oh, Dad!
We thank you a lot.
We pray for you
To the God.
Be happy a lot.

***

28. Dream

Yesterday, I had a dream that,
I was buying a cream.
The price of the cream was Rupees 100,
As it was a century, I thought,
I can't see clearly.
I went to buy spectacles
When,
I hit a wall.
My head blasted
And the blood flooded.
Oh! It was a bad dream
I would never go again to buy a cream.

***

29. My Mom

My mom, my mom,
I love you.
Please come, Please come,
I will serve you.
Mom, you gave me birth,
Mom, you live on Earth.
Mom, you give us food,
Mom, you are not our neighborhood.
But,
You are our loving mother
And you are so good.
Mom, I know, I know,
There is nothing for us that we love more than you
"I LOVE YOU, MOM".

***

30. Night

Night, night
It is bright.
The moon, the star
Are twinkling at the far.
There is no light,
But
The sky is bright.
We all see,
We know her,
She is the moon.
The twinkling ones,
That are many some are
The stars.

***

31. Smile

Smile when you are happy,
Smile when you are feeling sad,
Smile when you are with your friends,
Smile and don't feel bad.
Make others cheerful with this smile,
&
This smile will make you up in a while.

***

32. Elephants

The exciting elephant Thump! Thump! Thump!
Runs to her mother Clump! Clump! Clump!
Eating bananas Yumm! Yumm! Yumm!
Says to her mother Mom! Mom! Mom!
"I want more bananas"
Munching to a bunch
Crunch! Crunch! Crunch
The baby elephant Thump! Thump! Thump!

***

33. The Bare Tree

The tree behind the sea is fully bare,
Having no people to take care.
Who left it alone?
When it's standing like a clone.
If a child would swing in one try
He can say 'It's dry'.
The trees are weak,
Squeak, Squeak, Squeak.

***

34. The Brightest Star

The sun, the brightest star,
From us, it is very far.
It burns every day,
In the evening it is away.
It gives us light in the day,
But at night it does not stay.
Full of energy, full of light,
The sun is quite bright.

***

35. My Daddy

I like you
As you are brave
I like your confidence
When you save.
And I want it until I go grave.
You gave me all your love and support,
That's never-ending if I make a note.
For you and me the heart's the same.
I know about your name and fame.
I love you, Daddy.

***

36. The New Year

The brightest day
Comes in a year which let us
To cheer.
For fun to learn
It's all done.
Now let's say
Happy New Year!
With lots and lots of gay
On this beautiful day.
Let's welcome guys
To this year.
Write your resolutions.
Write your wishes.
Have lots of fun
And make your dishes.
&
Say "Happy new year"

***

37. Teacher

Oh, teacher!
You are the best creature,
Presented by God,
Or if any Lord….
You are a gift of God,
For making us big, big people,
Your blessings are always with me,
Thank you, teacher.

***

38. White

I am found in some flags
I am found in some papers
Who am I?
Can you guess me?
Yes, I am white.
I symbolise peace and calmness
That would melt your heart.
Never feel blue,
Be very calm and see me
I am white.

***

39. Red, Red, Red Colour

I am found in your blood,
I am available in nail polish,
I am there in some bags too.
I am everywhere,
I am the sign of danger.
But still, people love me.
And I am your favorite colour.

***

40. Silly Simon Saw A Spider

Silly Simon saw a spider,
That was up there on the top.
Silly Simon got scared
Of the tiny spider.
Silly Simon stood up and
Ran to the bedroom.
Let us make Silly Simon out of fear.

***

41. The Little girl In My Neighbourhood

The little girl in my neighbour,
Like the little sweet flavor.
She loves me, I love her,
Her name is Sai.
That is why, That is why,
We have a lot of fun,
And we are always done.
As my father always says,
"She is the first child of God".
She is the greatest gift for us
As my sister always fusses.

***

42. The Courageous Farmer

There was a farmer named Hari
In the village of Belam
Living in his farmhouse.
He was very happy with the animals.
Suddenly, a tornado came,
And destroyed the farmhouse.
They all started living in a cave
Which was under a mountain shade.
Then after 2 days,
When everything became alright,
They all helped the farmer
To build a new farmhouse
And lived happily ever after.

***

43. The Season

It may be summer or winter,
Winter or Autumn,
Autumn or Spring.
Spring will blossom flower's mum.
Every time it's a season,
Seasons are of many types,
Types like summer or winter or spring,
Spring or Autumn ripes.

***

44. The Sun

When the sun hides himself
And brings the night and bright sky,
Full of moon and stars
Smiling at the sun and greeting 'Hi'.
The moon gets happy
And plays with the stars,
Which twinkles brightly
At the night at very far.
The whole night shouting and howling,
And when the sun comes up
They say ' Goodbye' and go away.

***

45. What's In The River?

I saw a river,
It was long and blue as the sky.
There was a crocodile in the river,
He drank up a pond.
There was a fish,
Who stretched out of the earth.
There was a turtle,
Who slept for more than 10,000 years.
But,
An elephant which was the size of an ant
Bit my leg and I saw that
'That was a dream.

***

46. My Hero

Making me grow till this age,
Holding my hand and making me walk
Was a great memory with you.
I felt you pillow
When you sleep with me.
And you made me a purry cat.
The way I used to call you,
With different different names,
Which means the same meaning
In each and every frame.
I very much love you,
Which I till day felt.
I know you are my only dad and hero
Which I know very well.

***

47. Tree

Tree soars. It helps
Us in many ways. They are
The source of humans.
Giving us wood
And giving us food
Makes us happy
Than they would.

***

48. A Great Puzzle

The opened shelter becomes close
And asks me what have I chosen.
Then my mind couldn't be stable
And ran out away from the table.
Screaming and shouting
For the evil deeds,
To my heart
It again feeds.
Then it stops trying
When it sees everybody crying.
It can't understand the puzzle,
Which made it into great trouble.
Then my soul understood
And this was the end of the old trends.

***

49. First Day At School

When I woke up early,
The day was quite new and bright.
It was the first day of my school.
It was April 2,
And the day was very pleasant
I got ready quickly
To go to my school.
My father took me in his car,
And we reached the school.
I was a little timid
But still, I gathered my courage
And to my surprise
I saw my mom as my class teacher,
And then I spoke a lot.
All my shyness and timid went away
And I was there well to show off.

***

50. What If I Get A Magical Pen?

What if I get a magical pen?
I will get food for the poor,
I will get clothes for the four,
I will stop the lion's roar,
&
I will make the safety door.
I will draw many seeds,
I will give toys to many kids,
I will plant more trees,
And
I will make a forest which
Will give food to the poor for free.

***

9 798890 266477

Printed by Libri Plureos GmbH in Hamburg, Germany